914.7
CUM

COUNTRIES  OF THE WORLD

RUSSIA

Written and photographed by

David Cumming

Illustrated by Peter Bull

Wayland

Titles in this series

Australia	Italy
Brazil	Japan
Canada	The Netherlands
The Caribbean	New Zealand
China	Nigeria
France	Pakistan
Germany	Russia
Great Britain	Spain
Greece	The U.S.A.
India	West Germany

Cover *St Basil's Cathedral, Red Square, Moscow.*
Opposite *Country people often use bicycles to travel around locally.*

First published in 1994 by
Wayland (Publishers) Ltd
61 Western Road, Hove
East Sussex BN3 1JD, England

© Copyright 1994 Wayland (Publishers) Ltd

Editor: Katrina Maitland Smith & Paul Bennett
Series design: Malcolm Smythe
Book design: Marilyn Clay

British Library Cataloguing in Publication Data
Cumming, David
  Russia. – (Countries of the World Series)
  I. Title II. Bull, Peter III. Series
  914.7

  ISBN 0-7502-1314-0

Typeset by Dorchester Typesetting Group Ltd
Printed and bound in Italy by G. Canale and C.S.p.A., Turin

Contents

Words that appear in **bold** in the text are explained in the glossary on page 46.

1 New beginnings

Russia was once a small region in eastern Europe. Over the centuries its armies conquered northern Asia, until it controlled a huge empire containing many different peoples.

The Russian Empire was ruled by a royal family. In 1917 this family was overthrown and **communism** was introduced, with the Communist Party in charge of the **government**.

The Communist Party divided the empire into 15 **republics** within a country called the USSR (Union of Soviet Socialist Republics) or the Soviet Union. Russia was by far the biggest, richest and most powerful republic.

The Communist Party kept the USSR together, governing it strictly from Moscow, the capital city of both

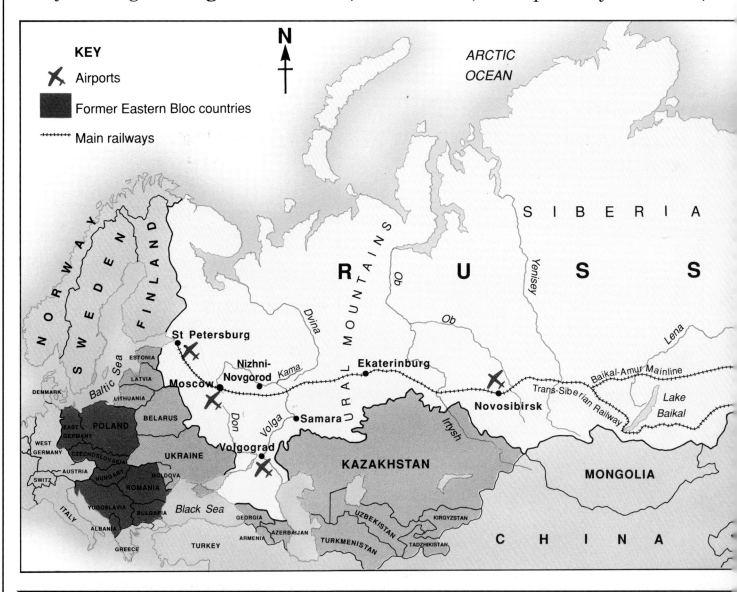

KEY

✈ Airports

▓ Former Eastern Bloc countries

++++++ Main railways

the USSR and the Russian republic. In 1991 the people of the USSR rebelled against the Communist Party and removed it from government. The same year, the republics became separate countries and the USSR ceased to exist. Each of the former republics changed to **capitalism** and introduced **democracy**. All but four are still linked because they are members of the CIS (**Commonwealth of Independent States**).

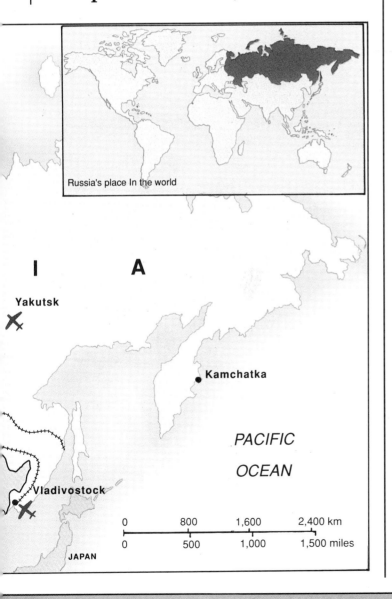

Russia's place In the world

I

A

Yakutsk

Kamchatka

PACIFIC

OCEAN

Vladivostock

| 0 | 800 | 1,600 | 2,400 km |

| 0 | 500 | 1,000 | 1,500 miles |

JAPAN

Communism turned the USSR into one of the most powerful countries in the world. However, it did not advance as fast as many of the capitalist countries. Industries and farms did not work well and much produce was wasted. People had less freedom in the USSR than in non-communist countries. The Communist Party controlled everything, from moving home to what was written in newspapers.

For most of its history, there was mistrust between the USSR and the non-communist countries (the West), led by the USA. Those days are over. Russia's former enemies are now helping it to become a democratic country with modern industries.

Russia is the biggest country in the world, occupying 17,100,000 sq km of land (almost the size of the USA and Canada put together). It stretches 11,250 km from the Baltic Sea in the west to the Pacific Ocean in the east, and is so wide that there are eleven **time zones** across the country. When it is midday in Moscow, for instance, it is 9 pm on the Pacific coast.

The Ural Mountains, running north to south, split Russia into two unequal parts. The majority of Russia's 148 million people live in the smaller part to the west of the Urals. Most of the industries and the best farming land is here too. On the eastern side of the Urals is Siberia, a huge region of forests, criss-crossed by rivers, which is covered with snow and ice for much of the year.

2 Land and climate

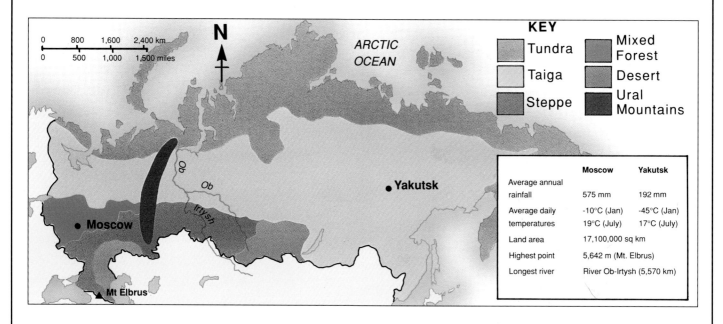

KEY

	Tundra		Mixed Forest
	Taiga		Desert
	Steppe		Ural Mountains

	Moscow	Yakutsk
Average annual rainfall	575 mm	192 mm
Average daily temperatures	-10°C (Jan) 19°C (July)	-45°C (Jan) 17°C (July)
Land area	17,100,000 sq km	
Highest point	5,642 m (Mt. Elbrus)	
Longest river	River Ob-Irtysh (5,570 km)	

Because Russia is so large, there are great variations in the country's landscape and climate.

To the west of the Ural Mountains there are huge, rolling plains. East of the Urals, the land is flat, but then rises gradually to the high mountains of eastern Siberia, which stretch to the shores of the Pacific. On the Kamchatka peninsula in the east, there are many active volcanoes. This is also an area where earthquakes often occur.

Russia has four different types of landscape. Along its northern edge, which is mainly within the Arctic Circle, there is the **tundra**. This is a region of shallow, poor soils where little grows except for lichens and mosses. Much of the ground is **permafrost**. It is frozen for most of the year.

South of the tundra is the **taiga**, a wide belt of **coniferous forests** across the centre of Russia. The most common trees are larch, pine, fir and spruce. The pine needles and cones falling from the trees make the soil acidic, so it is not good for farming.

A view of the taiga, the forests which cover central Russia from west to east.

Much of Russia has bitterly cold winters, with the ground covered with thick snow.

Further south of the taiga lies a band of flat grasslands called **steppe**. Its black soil, or *chernozem*, is excellent for farming.

South of the steppe, there is semi-desert. Little grows in the sandy soil here, unless it is well watered.

Most of Russia lies nearer the North Pole than the Equator. As a result much of the country has a very cold climate, with snow on the ground and ice on the seas, rivers and lakes for months at a time. The further east and north people live, the longer and colder are their winters. In north-eastern Siberia the temperature may drop to –70°C, making it the coldest inhabited place in the world. Summers here last only two or three months. During this time, the nights are short as the sun only sets for a few hours. In the winter, the opposite happens: the sun rises for two or three hours, so the nights are long.

Western Russia has shorter, less severe winters. Even so, temperatures frequently fall to –20°C and there is snow for three or four months, except in the far south of the country. This is the warmest part of Russia in winter and the hottest in summer, when temperatures can reach 35°C or higher.

The western part of Russia is the wettest area, with an annual rainfall of up to 800 mm. The south and north-east are the driest regions, with less than 400 mm of rain a year.

3 Wildlife

The wildlife of Russia is as varied as its landscape and climate. The tundra is home to polar bears and seals, which are able to withstand the bitterly cold winters.

Further south, reindeer, elk, wolves, bears, foxes, sable and ermine live in the taiga, along with many species of birds. The Siberian tiger, one of the rarest animals in Russia, can also be seen here.

Small **rodents** are the most common wildlife on the steppe and the neighbouring semi-desert lands. Large herds of bison, antelope, deer and wild horses once roamed the steppe. Except for a few deer, most have been killed by hunters armed with guns.

A number of animal species native to Russia have been hunted for centuries as much for their fur as for their meat. Worried that some species were facing **extinction**, the government published the *Red Book*, which lists all those in danger.

Left A colony of pelicans near the Black Sea, in southern Russia.

Below Jerboas can be seen in the semi-desert regions near the Caspian Sea.

Left The rare Siberian tiger – now, only 400 are thought to exist.

Below Majestic elk can be found in the taiga.

Hunting these is now forbidden. The government has also opened nature reserves where **endangered species** are encouraged to breed. The most successful reserve is at Prioksko-Terrasny, near Moscow, which has helped to save the European bison. This is Europe's and Russia's largest mammal. In the 1920s there were fewer than 50 of them; today there are over 3,000.

Pollution is now the main threat to Russia's wildlife. Lake Baikal, in southern Siberia, is the world's oldest and deepest lake. Once its water was clear enough to see to a depth of 40 m. Waste from a paper factory, built in the 1960s, has made this impossible today. The waste has also harmed the 2,000 plant and animal species living in and around the lake, many of which are found nowhere else.

The Russian government is trying to reduce the pollution caused by factories. But the equipment needed is expensive and neither the government nor the industries can afford to buy it. Although there are laws to stop pollution, few industries obey them.

4 Early years

In the first century AD, groups of **Slav** people left their traditional homelands in central and eastern Europe to settle along the rivers of what is now the Ukraine, on Russia's western border. Kiev became their biggest city. Life was difficult for the Slavs because they were raided constantly by **nomadic** peoples from central Asia. To escape them, some Slavs moved north and built another city, called Novgorod.

Soon they, too, were under attack. Early in the eighth century, Vikings from Scandinavia crossed the Baltic Sea in search of river routes to Constantinople (known today as Istanbul, in Turkey). This was an important trading city at the point where the Mediterranean enters the Black Sea.

The Vikings conquered Novgorod and the towns around it. The area controlled by them became known as 'Rus'. In 862, Rurik, a Viking leader, made himself Prince of Rus. He died shortly after and was succeeded by Oleg, a member of his family. Greedy for more land, Oleg attacked the town of Kiev in 882 and made it the capital of the new state of Rus, later to be called Russia.

In 1237 Russia was invaded by the Tartars (also known as the Mongols), a warlike people who were constantly in search of new lands to add to their

A painting of a traditional Mongol nomad village showing their tents or yurts.

A sixteenth-century Russian settlement.

huge empire. The Mongol army, the Golden Horde, was led by Batu Khan. He was the grandson of Genghis Khan, who had conquered much of China and central Asia earlier in the century. After Kiev was destroyed in 1240, Russia fell to the Tartars.

The Tartars ruled Russia for the next 200 years. In 1327 Ivan I, Prince of Moscow and a Slav, was given control of his city and its neighbouring lands in return for collecting taxes for his Tartar masters.

Moscow's princes became the most powerful in all Russia, and they made Moscow its capital. In 1480, Ivan III (or Ivan the Great as he was known) rebelled against the Tartars and defeated them. In 1547, his grandson, Ivan IV (nicknamed 'the Terrible'

because of his cruelty), crowned himself the **tsar**, or Emperor, of all Russia. His territory stretched across the north of what is now western Russia, from the Polish border to the Ural Mountains in the east.

Right *Ivan IV (nicknamed 'Ivan the Terrible'). He was the first Russian ruler to encourage British merchants to trade in Russia, which earned him another nickname, 'the English Tsar'.*

5 Modern times

The Russian people sold animal furs to pay the Tartars' taxes. After the Tartars' defeat in 1480, the trade in furs continued. By then there were so few animals left in Russia's forests that fur traders began hunting in the forests of Siberia.

Eager for more money and land, the tsars helped them by sending armies to conquer the peoples living there. In 1648 the Russian Empire reached the shores of the Pacific Ocean. Soon afterwards it was also extended south to the borders of present-day China.

From 1613, the tsars belonged to the Romanov family, which ruled Russia until 1917. The Romanovs were more interested in fighting wars than in improving living conditions in Russia. The people remained poor, uneducated and badly fed. In 1917 there was a **revolution** – the people rebelled and overthrew the tsar, then Nicholas II.

Russia, now renamed the USSR, became a communist country, ruled by the Communist Party. The USSR's first leader was Vladimir Ilyich Lenin, who put into practice many of the ideas of Karl Marx, the founder of Communism. Lenin died in 1924, and he was replaced by Joseph Stalin, who led the USSR until 1953.

Stalin was a cruel dictator, who put to death anyone who opposed his plans. Millions of people died.

One of the USSR's aims was to spread communism all over the world. The Western countries, led by the USA, believed that democracy and capitalism were better ways of running a country, so they did not approve of the USSR's plans.

Despite this, the USSR fought with the USA against Germany during the Second World War (1939–45). When peace came, the USSR occupied many of the countries in eastern Europe that had been conquered by Germany, and these countries became communist, too. Together, they became known as the **Eastern Bloc**.

Right Statues of Lenin can be seen all over the country. He was one of the leaders of the 1917 Revolution.

Above Tanks stand defiantly in Moscow's Red Square during the overthrow of the Communist Party in 1991.

This increased the mistrust between the USSR and the USA. An 'arms race' began as communist and democratic countries made sure they had enough weapons to prevent the other side invading them. This period became known as the 'Cold War' – a war of words in which neither side actually attacked the other.

The USA and Western Europe managed to become more wealthy at the same time as spending a lot of money on arms. The communist countries could not keep up with them. Their military forces had modern weapons, but there was little in the shops for their people to buy and no money to build new factories.

By the 1980s there was a big difference between life in democratic countries and in communist ones. One by one, the countries of the Eastern Bloc rebelled successfully against the Communist Party. In 1991 the Party was overthrown in the USSR, and the USSR was split into 15 countries.

Important dates

862	Rurik became Prince of Novgorod-Rus.
882	Oleg conquered Kiev and founded Rus, later to be called Russia.
1240	Kiev destroyed by the Tartars.
1480	Ivan the Great defeated the Tartars. Moscow now the capital city.
1547	Ivan the Terrible became first tsar.
1613	Michael, the first Romanov tsar, crowned.
1712	St Petersburg became Russian capital.
1812	Napoleon Bonaparte invaded Russia unsuccessfully.
1917	Tsar Nicholas II gave up the throne. Russia renamed the USSR and ruled by the Communist Party, led by Lenin.
1918	Moscow became the capital again.
1924-53	USSR ruled by Stalin.
1945	At the end of the Second World War, the USSR brought communism to eastern European countries.
1940s 1980s	Cold War of words between the USSR and the USA.
1989	Anti-communist revolution in Poland led to the overthrow of the Communist Party in other eastern European countries.
1991	Communism ended in the USSR. USSR split into 15 countries, all but four of which remain linked by the CIS.

6 The people

Most foreigners think that everyone in Russia is a Russian, but this is not so. Millions of people in Russia would be offended if they were called Russians.

Although the Vikings helped to create the original Russia, most of the people living there were Slavs, and Slavic princes and then tsars became its rulers. Armies of Slavic soldiers invaded and conquered new lands for the Russian Empire and the inhabitants of these lands reluctantly became citizens of Russia.

Above This Slavic woman decided to leave Uzbekistan because Russians are now unpopular there.

This father and his sons are 'proper Russians'. They are descendants of the Slavs from Eastern Europe.

Within Russia today, there are over 100 different peoples, such as the Avars, Kalmyks, Ossetians, Chechens and Chuvash. If you ask any of them who they are, they will reply that they are Kalmyks or Chechens, and not Russians.

The only people it is correct to call Russians are the descendants of the Slavs. They are the biggest group, making up nearly 82 per cent of the population (121 million people). The 5.5 million Tartars in central Russia are the largest group after the Russians. They make up 4 per cent of the population. Their ancestors came with Batu Khan's army. The Aleuts, fishing people on Siberia's Pacific coast, are the smallest group. There are fewer than 500 of them.

The Russians have little in common with many of the non-Slavic peoples. Non-Slavic peoples often have a different appearance, language, customs and religion. For example, the Tartars of western Russia are **Muslims**, while the Buryats of southern Siberia are **Buddhists**.

Because the non-Slavic people were different and did not like their conquerors, the Russians have always feared they would rebel. To prevent this happening, the tsars encouraged Russians to move to new lands, where they were given all the important jobs. The Communist Party continued to ensure that Russians were more powerful than local peoples. The Russians treated the local peoples badly and forced them to live like Russian people.

In recent years the non-Slavic peoples have been given more freedom to run their own affairs.

Russia has been divided up according to the borders of the traditional homelands of the largest groups of peoples. There are 16 republics, 5 regions and 10 areas. Although there are more Russians than local peoples in these territories, the Russians no longer have all the power. The local peoples have important jobs in government and they have started to put right the unfair laws made by Russians.

Above *This boy's ancestors came from central Asia.*

Left *Most of these children are descended from people conquered by the Russians.*

7 Language

Above Russian film posters. The words are made up of letters from the Cyrillic alphabet.

There are almost as many languages in Russia as there are different peoples. Some are only spoken by a few thousand people; others, like the Turkic language of the Tartars, are spoken by a few million. To prevent confusion, Russian is the official language throughout the country. The Communist Party did not like local peoples speaking their own languages and it allowed only Russian to be taught in schools. Today, local languages are taught once again and are used in signs and newspapers.

Russian is one of the most widely spoken languages in the world, along with English, Chinese and Spanish. Besides being the main language of the 148 million people living in Russia, it is also spoken by about 102 million people in the other countries of the CIS.

Russian, like English, comes from an ancient group of languages known as Indo-European. The fact that Russian and English are related means that they have words in common. For instance, the Russian for sister is *syestra*, and *tri* is the number three. These words only look familiar when they are spelt with English letters. Written in Russian, they would look very strange indeed.

The Russian alphabet is called Cyrillic. It is named after St Cyril, a Greek missionary who went to Russia in the ninth century AD to teach Christianity. Since the people of Russia had no alphabet, St Cyril was unable to translate the Bible for them to read. So he invented his own alphabet. It has thirty-three letters, most of which were borrowed from the Greek alphabet. However, some were taken from **Latin**, which is why they are the same as English letters.

Russian is not an easy language to learn: even Russians find the **grammar** very complicated. Nevertheless, they are very proud of it and make good use of its huge **vocabulary**. Newspapers and magazines are full of fine writing, and politicians and business people make speeches showing off their excellent command of the language.

Russia's Cyrillic Alphabet

RUSSIAN	ENGLISH		RUSSIAN	ENGLISH	
а	a	father	р	r	run
б	b	but	с	s	sing
в	v	van	т	t	ten
г	g	got	у	u	food
д	d	dog	ф	f	fan
е	ye	yet	х	kh	loch
ё	yo	your	ц	ts	bits
ж	zh	treasure	ч	ch	chin
з	z	zoo	ш	sh	shop
и	i	meet	щ	shch	fresh
й	y	yellow	ъ		(silent)
к	k	kind	ы	y	ill
л	l	long	ь		(silent)
м	m	mad	э	e	end
н	n	not	ю	yu	use
о	o	more	я	ya	yard
п	p	pig			

Above The alphabet created by St Cyril has thirty-three letters – seven more than in the alphabet we use.

Left Comics like this are very new in Russia, and children enjoy reading them.

8 Religion and festivals

Most people in Russia are Christians who belong to the Russian Orthodox Church. Its teachings are similar to those of the Greek Orthodox Church, which sent St Cyril to Russia in the ninth century AD to convert the people to Christianity.

After Christianity, the most important religion in Russia is Islam. This was brought to Russia in the thirteenth century by the Tartar armies led by Batu Khan. Their descendants are still Muslims and the mosques in which they pray can be seen in the cities where they live.

Above Jews are starting to worship again in their synagogues after being forbidden under communism.

Destroyed by the Communists, this Moscow church is now being rebuilt.

In towns and cities you can also see the synagogues used by Jews, and along the eastern shores of Lake Baikal in southern Siberia, the Buddhist Buryats have built their temples. In central Siberia, native peoples such as the Evenki and Yakuts are known as animists. They believe that good and evil spirits exist in the natural world around them. They try to control these spirits through priests called *shamans*.

After the 1917 Revolution which overthrew the last tsar, the Communist Party made the USSR an **atheist** country. It discouraged people from following their religions and closed most places of worship. People who continued to practise their religions got into a lot of trouble.

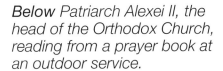

Right Many pilgrims visit St Sergius Monastery, Zagorsk, because it is the most important place in the Russian Orthodox Church.

Below Patriarch Alexei II, the head of the Orthodox Church, reading from a prayer book at an outdoor service.

After 1917 all traditional religious festivals were banned. They were replaced with holidays to celebrate important events in the USSR's history, such as the anniversary of the Revolution. Since the USSR was created for the good of its people, whose wishes had been ignored in tsarist times, there were also holidays in honour of ordinary citizens, such as 1 May (May Day) for workers and 8 March, Women's Day.

After the break-up of the USSR, people of all faiths have been allowed to worship and to celebrate religious festivals again. In communist times, Christmas Day was replaced with a holiday on New Year's Day, 1 January. Today, people still work at Christmas and continue to give presents and hold big parties at New Year. Easter is the most important occasion in the Russian Orthodox Church. There are special services and children decorate eggs with colourful designs. For Muslims, Ramadan, a month of fasting, is an important time.

There are many seasonal festivals all over the country. In the north-east, the end of winter is marked with ski and reindeer races. In Siberia, the Yakuts have a summer festival, called *Ysyakh*, with horse-races, wrestling matches and traditional singing and dancing.

9 Country life

Under the tsars, Russia was a land of villages. At the time of the 1917 Revolution, over 80 per cent of the population lived in the countryside. When the USSR broke up in 1991, this figure had fallen to less than 40 per cent. By the year 2000 it is expected to be nearer 25 per cent. People have left the countryside because life there is very hard and there are few opportunities for work.

Most villages are built along a single street, with a row of houses on either side. The street is usually a track, which turns into a muddy mess when the snow thaws or after rain.

The houses are single-storey wooden cottages, often prettily decorated with painted shutters and carved window frames. Inside, the rooms are small and there is little furniture. Old cottages are heated by a huge oven in the kitchen which pokes through the wall into one of the bedrooms. It is wide enough for people to sleep on during cold winter nights.

Typical village houses in southern Russia. The wood pile will be used for heating in winter.

Above Village children are luckier than city children because their homes have gardens in which to play.

Left Village people selling fruit and vegetables grown in their kitchen gardens.

Nearly every village now has electricity, so most families have televisions, radios and refrigerators, but only a few have a telephone. Most cottages have no running water. Instead of a bathroom, families have a **sauna** to keep clean. The sauna is in a shed at the bottom of the garden, near the toilet.

Larger villages have a small school and one or two shops, but the choice of things to buy is very limited. Most families grow all the vegetables they need on land near their homes. Meat is bought from local people who keep farm animals.

Country life is toughest for the people of Siberia. This region is often described as a huge, empty space because little has been done to develop it. Nearly one-and-a-half-times larger than the USA, Siberia has 24 million inhabitants, which is only about one-tenth of the USA's population. Few people want to live there because conditions are so unpleasant. Most of the people live in villages scattered far and wide. The winters are long, with temperatures dropping far below freezing-point for months on end. Strong winds from the Arctic whip up the snow, making travel impossible on the bad roads and cutting off villages for weeks at a time. In winter, the sun only appears for two or three hours. Summers are short, but the days are long, as the sun sets for only a few hours. The hot sun melts the top layer of frozen earth, turning it into marshes swarming with mosquitoes and flies.

Above *Most country people can grow all their vegetables, so they need not buy them.*

Below *Few people want to live in Siberia because of its harsh climate – winters are long and cold; summers, short and hot.*

A group of Siberian reindeer herders in front of their yurt *home.*

The freezing and thawing of the ground can cause the wooden houses to tilt and even to collapse.

Many of the native peoples of Siberia are reindeer herders. They live in houses only in the winter when it is too cold to work outside. In the spring and summer, they live in tents, called *yurts*, while they move around, taking their animals to fresh pastures.

In recent years the government has tried to encourage people to stay in the countryside by improving conditions in the villages. New schools, roads, and houses with central heating have been built. There are also new meeting-halls which can be used for plays and film shows. Remote villages have been connected to gas and electricity supplies. Yet many people would still prefer to move to a city if they were given the opportunity.

10 City life

Modern and old blocks of flats on the outskirts of Moscow.

During tsarist times Russia had fallen behind the other developing countries in Europe. The Communist Party wanted the USSR to catch up, so it began building cities and industries. Nearly 50 per cent of Russia's cities, and most of its factories, have been built since 1917. Millions of people left the countryside to work in the new cities, where they thought life would be easier and better for them.

Huge tower blocks were erected to provide homes for these people. They were all designed in the same style and made out of concrete slabs, which meant they could be put up quickly and cheaply. All the flats were small so that the tower blocks could contain as many as possible.

Although thousands of tower blocks have been built, there are still not enough homes in the cities. Grandparents have to live with their children, and newly married couples have to remain with their parents. Families of five or six people often have to share a flat consisting of a living-room, bedroom and tiny kitchen and bathroom. At night the living-room is used as another bedroom. The flats are cluttered with furniture and possessions, so the balcony has to be used for storage space. It is common to see bicycles and sledges hanging from the balcony railings, along with washed clothes.

Recently, the shortage of housing has been made worse by the return of Russian soldiers and their families from former Eastern Bloc countries, where they are no longer wanted. **Refugees** from wars in countries along Russia's borders, such as Armenia and Georgia, have also added to the shortage problem.

In many cities, people now own their flats. Previously flats belonged to the state, which charged a low rent from people living in them. Since 1991, the government has been giving free flats to the people, so they do not need to borrow money to buy them.

Above There are not enough flats, so children continue to live with their parents after they are married.

Most blocks of flats have areas where children can play outside in the summer.

Today, the owners of flats pay for the upkeep of their block, as well as for heating and electricity and gas. In the future, though, the government plans to tax people who own their flats.

Most flats are of a low standard because they were built quickly and as cheaply as possible. They all have double-glazed windows to keep out the cold, and central heating. The Communist Party considered it cheaper and more efficient to pipe hot water to the tower blocks from power stations rather than to provide individual flats with boilers. If these break down or the pipes leak, hundreds of families are affected. Hot water is supplied all year, but the city government decides when to switch the heating on and off. In most cities it starts on 1 October and stops at the end of April.

In the USSR, the state owned all the land, so it was quite easy to plan the development of the new cities. It was decided to house people on the outskirts of cities in huge estates. As well as blocks of flats, these estates had plenty of open spaces, shops and schools. To reduce the shortage of homes, many more flats were built than was originally planned. Today, the estates are crowded and there are often not enough shops, schools and play areas for all the families living on them.

The centre of every city has been planned around a large square, which can be used for parades on public holidays and other special occasions. Surrounding the square are government buildings, parks, museums, cinemas and theatres. The city planners wanted to show that this was the 'heart' of the city: the place where all the important decisions were made, as well as the place where people would come to enjoy themselves, either in the open air or at an exhibition or a film.

Leading off the central square are streets full of shops. Russian shops do not have eye-catching window displays or colourful signs outside to attract shoppers. Inside, the decoration and lighting are poor and the choice of goods is limited.

Above Winter sports on an ice-covered square in the centre of Moscow.

Right Department stores have opened in cities in recent years. Most of them have only a limited choice of goods for sale.

Left In the summer, people buy fruit and vegetables at open-air markets. In the winter the stalls are indoors.

Below Many of the books on sale here were banned by the Communist Party because they showed that life was better under capitalism.

However, in the big cities, such as Moscow and St Petersburg, things are changing quickly. Under communism, all the shops were owned by the state, which cared little about what was on offer or how goods were presented. Today, many shops are run by both Russian and foreign firms, competing with each other for people's money. Their shops are modern and they have a wide variety of goods on sale, many of which were unobtainable a few years ago. Some of the firms are opening supermarkets and department stores.

In the centre of every city there is a large market, where people can buy fresh fruit and vegetables from local farmers. Shoppers can also buy things from pavement sellers. Some have stalls, perhaps with books or toys. Others are poor people with only one or two items to sell.

Russians buy everything with cash. They do not have cheque books and credit cards. But in Moscow and St Petersburg this is changing. Rich businesspeople now have credit cards.

11 Education

By law, all children must go to school for ten years, from the age of six until they are sixteen years old. Before starting school, many children are sent to a **kindergarten** because both their parents are out at work all day.

Most schools are run by the government. The top government schools are called *gymnasiums*. They charge a small amount for fees and have an entrance exam which pupils have to pass before they are admitted. All the other government schools have no entrance exams. They are free, but conditions in them are not as good as in the *gymnasiums*. The classes are larger and there is less equipment. The children are taught fewer subjects than in a *gymnasium*, where it is possible to learn music or a foreign language, such as English, French or Spanish.

Private schools are now allowed to open in Russia. There are few of them because the fees are so high that only the richest families can afford them. Private schools give children the best education.

Nearly all school teachers are women. During communist times, teachers often had to give their classes inaccurate information because the Communist Party wanted children to think that life in democratic countries was worse than in the USSR. Today, teachers are free to tell the truth about what is happening in Russia and abroad.

These children will get good jobs because they are being taught well at a gymnasium *school.*

All schools are mixed, with boys and girls in the same class. There are no uniforms – children wear their everyday clothes.

Children go to school from Monday to Friday. Lessons start at 8.30 in the morning and last until 3 o'clock in the afternoon, although young children go home at lunchtime. Some parents have the money to pay for their children to have extra classes after school. This used to be forbidden, but now it is quite common.

Above All but the youngest children are given homework – the older they are, the more they get.

The main building of Moscow University, one of the best and biggest universities in Russia.

All over Russia, the school year begins on 1 September, when the buses and trams are full of children carrying little presents and bunches of flowers for their teachers. Most of that day is spent in the parks, where activities and games have been organized to celebrate the return to school. School lessons start on 2 September. The school year ends on 31 May and teachers and pupils have a three-month holiday. There are also short holidays at the Christian festivals of Christmas and Easter.

After ten years in school, pupils have a choice about their futures. They can continue their studies and, if they pass an exam, can go on to university. They can move to a college to learn a skill, such as engineering or woodworking, or they can leave school and find a job.

12 Food and drink

In the morning people are usually in too much of a hurry to make a big breakfast. It is a simple, quick meal: perhaps a boiled egg, some cold meats and bread, all washed down with sweetened tea without milk. Russians make a pot of strong tea, pour a little into a cup, then add boiling water. The water used to be heated in a **samovar**, but nowadays a kettle is used. Many Russians drink herbal teas, sweetening them with spoonfuls of homemade jam.

Lunch is the main meal of the day. Most people eat lunch in the canteens of their offices or factories. They begin with a bowl of soup, followed with a plate of chicken or meat, usually in a thick gravy, accompanied by buckwheat, rice or potatoes and a salad.

In winter, the soup will be hot, like the traditional *borscht*, made from beetroots, onions and meat. In summer, cold yoghurt soups, full of chopped-up vegetables, are a favourite. For dessert, people often eat pancakes, called *blinys*, with a fruit or sour cream filling. In summer, people drink *compote* with their lunch. It is the juice of stewed fruits with water added to it.

Above In the summer, people enjoy eating shashlik, barbecued mutton, at home or on the street.

Left Sweets, cakes, and water heated in a samovar, *all make up a traditional afternoon tea.*

The evening meal is light. It is often a selection of cold dishes, like smoked sausages and salted or pickled fish, or a hot dish, such as the traditional *pelmeni*, which is similar to ravioli.

In the summer, people eat a lot of fruit and vegetables, most of which come from the gardens of their country cottages, called **dachas**. In the summer, too, families **pickle** enough vegetables to last them through the winter when fresh crops are scarce because nothing can grow in the frozen ground.

During the summer, people have barbecues at their *dachas*, when they cook *shashlik*, chunks of mutton on skewers. *Shashlik* sellers can also be seen in the parks and on street corners. Summers are hot all over Russia and people get very thirsty.

Above Russians of all ages love ice-cream, especially during the hot summer months.

People queuing to buy a glass of kvass on a hot summer's day.

When they are out and about, they drink *kvass*, which is made from dark, rye bread and tastes like beer. It contains no alcohol, so children enjoy it just as much as adults. A lot of ice-creams are sold in summer and almost as many in winter, even when the temperature is below freezing.

Most Russian people are overweight because their diet is poor. They eat a lot of fried food and sweet pastries, cakes and puddings. Some men drink too much vodka and beer, and many become **alcoholics**. In the late 1980s, President Gorbachev banned the sale of vodka to reduce drunkenness. This made him so unpopular that he was forced to withdraw his ban.

13 Sport and leisure

The Communist Party wanted the USSR's sportsmen and women to be the best in the world, so a lot of time and money was spent training them. As a result, the USSR won many gold medals in the Olympics and its teams were the champions in international sports competitions. To encourage people to take up sports, the Communist Party built stadiums, swimming-pools and sports halls. Today, Russia's cities are well equipped with sports facilities which everyone can use.

The most popular sports are football, ice hockey and basketball. In winter, ponds, lakes and rivers freeze over with ice which is thick enough for people to skate on safely. Children also enjoy tobogganing down the snow-covered slopes.

Above Football is the most popular spectator sport and loyal fans never miss a home match.

Below In winter there is always enough snow for people to go tobogganing.

Left Boys fishing in the river beside their dacha *outside Moscow, where they spend most weekends in summer.*

Below People cooling off in the River Volga, in southern Russia, on a hot summer's day.

During the summer most families spend the weekends at their *dachas*, many of which have been built in forests or near lakes and rivers, so there are plenty of opportunities for walking and water sports. Each *dacha* usually has a large garden, or an allotment near by, where fruit and vegetables are grown. People spend a lot of time taking care of the plants and trees.

The Communist Party built children's holiday camps outside cities and hotels and health spas along the coast of the Black Sea. Many of the camps now belong to businesses, and workers can send their children to them in the summer for little cost.

The Black Sea holiday resorts were once free to members of the Communist Party. Today, people have to pay to stay in them, and the prices are too high for all but the most well off families.

In summer, people like to spend most of their time outdoors to take advantage of the warm, light evenings. In winter, most evenings are spent at home, watching television. Many families now have video machines. There are no video libraries yet, but 'pirate' tapes (illegal copies) are often on sale. In big cities, such as Moscow and St Petersburg, there are nightclubs, casinos and discos for those who are rich enough to afford them.

14 Arts and crafts

The nineteenth century was the golden age of Russian culture. Many major works in Russian literature and music were produced then, and their creators became famous not only in Russia, but all over the world. Important people from this time include: the poet, Alexander Pushkin (1799–1837); the novelists, Ivan Turgenev (1818–83), Fyodor Dostoevsky (1821–81) and Leo Tolstoy (1828–1910); the playwright, Anton Chekhov (1860–1904); and the composers, Modest Mussorgsky (1839–81) and Peter Tchaikovsky (1840–93). Ballet flourished and Russian ballet dancers were soon among the best in the world, a position which they occupy today.

Above Visitors to Moscow having their portrait drawn by one of the many artists in the city.

Left Woodcarving is a centuries-old tradition. This figure was carved in eastern Siberia.

After the 1917 Revolution, life became very difficult for writers, musicians and artists in the USSR. The Communist Party wanted them to practise the official communist art, called **Socialist Realism**. Music, books, films, paintings, sculptures all had to celebrate communist life. Anything that criticized communism was banned and its creator punished, often by being sent to a remote part of Siberia.

Today, Russians are free to express themselves in any way they want. Books which were once banned are on sale. Previously censored films can be shown without the cuts the Communist Party demanded. Artists can paint in their individual styles once again.

Right Lacquered boxes decorated with miniature paintings, another old handicraft in Russia.

Below Colourful traditional costumes clothe these dolls, which have been made for tourist souvenirs.

Long before television, there was little to do during the long, dark winters, so people practised a craft. The skills learned centuries ago have been passed on and are used today, although machines do much of the work previously done by hand. Surrounded by thick pine forests, many people became expert woodcarvers. Their descendants now make toys, including *matryoshka* dolls (which slot inside each other); pine cups and bowls, coloured red, black and gold; and boxes decorated with detailed paintings. Potters in Gzhel, near Moscow, remain famous for the blue-and-white pottery first produced in the 1700s. In Rostov-Veliky, also close to Moscow, craftsmen continue to make *finift* (miniature paintings on metal), using processes first discovered over two hundred years ago.

15 Farming

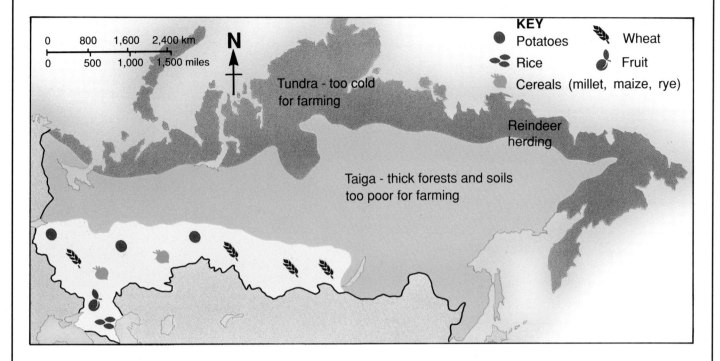

KEY
- ● Potatoes
- ◆ Rice
- 🌾 Wheat
- ● Fruit
- ● Cereals (millet, maize, rye)

Tundra - too cold for farming

Reindeer herding

Taiga - thick forests and soils too poor for farming

0   800   1,600   2,400 km
0   500   1,000   1,500 miles

N

Although Russia has a lot of land, less than a quarter can be used for farming. Most farming land is in the western half of the country and south-western Siberia. The rest of the land cannot be used, either because the climate is too cold or the soils are too poor. The main crops are wheat, barley, rye and sugar beet. Cattle, pigs, sheep and goats are also reared on farms. With only a relatively small area of land available for farming, feeding the population has always been a problem.

At the time of the 1917 Revolution, Russia had many small, private farms which were unable to grow enough food for people in the towns and cities as well as for those in the countryside. Widespread hunger in the cities was an important cause of the last tsar's downfall. To increase food production, the state became the owner of all the land in the USSR. In the late 1920s the communist government reorganized agriculture by 'collectivization', joining together about 100 farms into a single, large farm, called a collective or *kolkhoz*.

On a *kolkhoz*, people work in teams, ploughing, planting and harvesting. Each *kolkhoz* has a mixture of crops and animals, and everything it produces is bought by the government. The more a *kolkhoz* produces, the higher the price the government pays for its crops or animals. All the *kolkhoz*'s earnings are shared equally between the different farm workers.

The government also created *sovkhoz* farms. There are fewer of these but they are bigger than a *kolkhoz* and specialize in one crop or one breed of animal. *Sovkhoz* workers are paid a wage, like factory workers.

On both *kolkhoz* and *sovkhoz* the government provides all the machinery, fertilizers and seeds. Workers are given a small plot of land to cultivate themselves, and they can sell the fruit and vegetables they produce in markets.

Despite these changes, not enough food has been produced by the farms. They have been run badly and lack good equipment. In recent years, the government has had to buy food from other countries to make up for the shortages in the cities.

Kolkhoz *farm workers hitching a lift on a tractor carrying sacks of fertilizer.*

However, the farm workers have produced a lot of food on their plots of land. The USSR's government realized that farmers took more care of crops if they felt they were working for themselves. Today farmers are encouraged to rent land and farm machinery from the government and to grow crops which they can then sell themselves both to the government and in markets.

Nevertheless, even if more food is produced, much of it is rotten by the time it reaches the cities. The government needs to improve transport and the way fruit and vegetables are distributed to prevent this happening in the future.

Left A farmer taking his cows home to be milked. He can sell the milk afterwards.

16 Industry

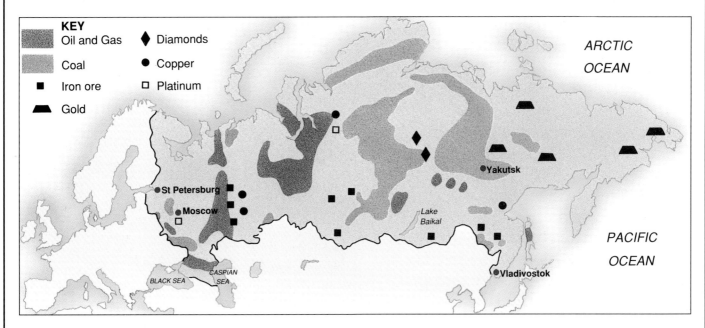

KEY
- Oil and Gas
- Coal
- Iron ore
- Gold
- ◆ Diamonds
- ● Copper
- □ Platinum

ARCTIC OCEAN

St Petersburg
Moscow
Yakutsk
Lake Baikal
Vladivostok

BLACK SEA
CASPIAN SEA

PACIFIC OCEAN

Russia was very backward in 1917. Compared with Europe and the USA, it had few industries. Within fifty years, communism had turned the country into one of the most important industrial nations in the world.

The communists were able to do this because they created a 'command economy' in which the state owned everything, from the factories to the minerals in the ground, and governments gave orders about how these resources should be used.

Governments made **Five-Year Plans** which showed what types of factories would be built and how much they would produce. Until recently, all the plans gave priority to 'heavy industries', such as iron and steel and engineering. Defence industries, too, expanded fast because governments wanted strong armed forces to protect the USSR and the Eastern Bloc countries from invasion.

By the 1960s the USSR was falling behind other countries again. The USSR had huge supplies of resources, such as coal, oil, gas, iron ore and precious metals, but they were not being used to the country's advantage. So much money was spent on making weapons that other industries were suffering. Many factories were out of date but there was no money to modernize them. Neither was there enough money to produce all the things people wanted for their homes and everyday life. The USSR could not earn extra money through trade because other countries did not want to buy its goods, which were badly made and old fashioned.

When Mikhail Gorbachev became President of the USSR in 1985, he decided to end the mistrust that had existed between communist and capitalist countries since the end of the Second World War in 1945. He made agreements with the USA and Europe to reduce the amount of money being spent on arms. He also began to change the way industries were run in his country. Although the USSR remained a command economy, capitalist ideas were introduced to make industries more efficient. Instead of carrying out the orders of government officials in Moscow,

Above This steel factory in Volgograd has old-fashioned machines because the Communist Party had no money to modernize it.

Below This shipyard on the River Volga is finding it difficult to compete with foreign-owned shipyards, so it may have to close.

factory managers began to make their own decisions about prices and about how much and what to produce. US and European firms, previously kept out of the USSR, were encouraged to do business there. All these changes were part of a process called ***perestroika***.

Today, Russia wants to be a capitalist country with a **market economy** in which most industries will be run by businesspeople and not by the government. Many factories have already been sold to private companies. Others have had to close down because the government will no longer help them with money. Yet others can only continue because foreign companies are providing them with modern equipment. The change from a command economy to a market economy will take many years and cause many problems.

17 Transport

Left Most families do not have a car, so they travel around on public transport. Many cities have electrically powered trolley-buses, like this one.

The Communist Party considered cars a wasteful use of precious resources. It thought that money and time was better spent on building trucks, trains, and buses. Consequently, very few cars were made in the USSR. Even the cheapest cars cost as much as workers earned in three years. Today, more cars are available but they remain very expensive. Only one in three families can afford one, so most people have to rely on public transport to travel about.

The public transport system is large and the fares are cheap, but it is very crowded because so many people have to use it to get to work and to go shopping. Within towns and cities there are buses, trolley buses, trams and taxis. In big cities, such as Moscow and St Petersburg, there are also good underground train services. The underground in Moscow has over 100 stations and carries 5 million passengers every day.

Buses connect towns and cities with nearby villages. In the countryside, people use motorbikes and bicycles for short journeys.

The Communist Party built railways rather than roads to help new industries, since trains were a better way to move goods over long distances. To bring Siberia's minerals to the factories in the west, the Trans-Siberian railway was built early this century. It is the longest railway line in the world, stretching 9,300 km from Moscow to Vladivostock, on the Pacific coast.

Russia is such a huge country that travelling by train takes a long time.

Above Planes connect remote villages in Siberia with the nearest city.

For example, the journey from Moscow to Vladivostock takes eight days. So that people could move about quickly, the Communist Party built many airports and kept the price of plane tickets low. The USSR soon had the biggest airline in the world, called Aeroflot. In Siberia there are few roads and railways because the climate makes them very expensive, if not impossible, to construct. Aeroflot's planes and helicopters are the only way in which many Siberian villages can keep in touch with the rest of the country. Flying around Russia was very cheap in communist times but, today, prices are higher and fewer people travel by plane.

Russia has 140,000 km of rivers and canals which can be used for transport, but most of them are frozen

Below A sledge is the best way of travelling in Siberia during the winter months when roads are covered with snow and ice.

for at least three months of the year. As a result, goods are carried by road and rail, which are open throughout the year. Much of the oil and gas is transported by pipeline. Some of it is taken across Russia to Europe.

18 Government

For most of its history, the USSR was run by the Communist Party. It controlled everything, from what laws were passed to what was seen on television. It was able to do this because all other political parties were banned by the USSR's **constitution**. At elections, people could only vote for members of the Communist Party. As a result, everyone in the government and in the Parliament was a communist. The USSR's leader was also the leader of the Communist Party. In everyday life, membership of the Communist Party was necessary for workers to get good jobs. The Communist Party believed that strict control was the only way to keep together a country as large as the USSR, which also contained so many different peoples.

When Mikhail Gorbachev became president of the USSR in 1985, he gave the people more freedom to say what they wanted. He called this *glasnost*, meaning openness or truthfulness. Gorbachev also made elections more democratic by allowing the people to vote for non-communists to be elected to the Parliament.

Gorbachev's introduction of democracy was extended further in 1990, when the USSR's constitution was changed to allow political parties other than the Communist Party to exist. In 1991 the Communist Party lost all its power. People no longer needed to be communists to hold important jobs.

After the end of the USSR, its current president, Boris Yeltsin, remained president of Russia, the

The Kremlin in Moscow houses the offices of the most important people in the Russian government.

Right This used to be the Russian Parliament. It was attacked by the army in October 1993 when some of its members rebelled against President Yeltsin (**above**). A new Parliament is now being built.

new country. He wanted to make Russia more democratic and to become a capitalist country in which private businesses were more important than state businesses. His plans to alter Russia were blocked by Parliament, where there were still many communists who did not want change. In September 1993, Yeltsin closed Parliament and ordered elections, in which the people would also vote to accept or reject his new constitution. In December 1993, Yeltsin's constitution was accepted.

In this new constitution, Russia will have a president elected by the people every four years. The next presidential elections are scheduled for 1996. The president appoints the prime minister, who chooses the members of the government after discussions with the president. The prime minister and the government are responsible for the everyday running of Russia. They are watched over by the Parliament, whose members are elected by the people.

In December 1993 the people voted for the first time in democratic elections in which 13 political parties fought for seats in the new Parliament. Russia's Choice, the party which supports President Yeltsin, won fewer seats than the Liberal Democratic Party, which opposes his plans to reform Russia. Many people now fear that the new constitution makes the president so powerful that he will close Parliament again and govern without it. If this happens, some people say that democracy in Russia will come to an end and one man, and the political party supporting him, will rule the country much like old communist times in the USSR.

19 Facing the future

Life is very hard for people in Russia today. In communist times, the government gave money to industries and farmers to help them keep prices low, so that things were relatively cheap to buy. The government no longer provides any help because it is short of money. As a result, the prices of many everyday items have been rising every month, even though the wages people earn have stayed the same. Some government factories do not even have enough money to pay their workers. Families have had to cut back on what they buy to survive.

Above *Goods which were not available in the USSR are on sale now in Russia.*

Under communism, there was no unemployment. The money the government gave to industries kept all factories open, even if they were badly run. Without that money, many factories are having to shut, leaving thousands of workers without jobs.

The USSR did most of its trading with the Eastern Bloc. Much of the business was by barter: goods were swapped between countries rather than bought and sold. Today, Russia wants to trade all over the world. It will have to compete with industries in other countries to produce goods of high quality at low prices. Many of Russia's old factories will have to modernize. Their managers and workers need to learn new skills.

Above *Tourism will be an important industry in the future because many people want to visit Russia.*

Russia does not have enough money to do all this on its own, so other countries have agreed to help. They have promised $24 billion. However, probably ten or twenty times that amount will be needed, because new banks, offices, computers and communications systems will have to be built so that foreign firms can do business with Russia.

Many of the peoples living in Russia are unhappy about the way they have been treated in the past. The largest groups occupy their own regions within Russia where they can decide things for themselves. Now, some of the peoples want to turn their regions into separate countries. The Yakut people of Yakutia, in Siberia, want to do this. However, they are outnumbered by Russians (who are descendants of the Slavs), many of whom say they would leave Yakutia for Russia if Yakutia became independent. The arrival of these people would create extra problems in Russia, where there is already a shortage of jobs and houses.

Russia has very large supplies of minerals and energy. It has one-third of the world's gas, and huge amounts of oil, coal, iron ore, gold, silver and diamonds. In the USSR, these natural resources were used inefficiently. With the help of foreign firms and governments, they can be used to good effect so that Russia will be a rich country in the next century, with life becoming easier for all its people.

A long queue outside a new American clothing shop in the centre of Moscow.

Glossary

Alcoholics   People who are dependent on drinking alcoholic drinks.

Atheist   Someone who believes that God does not exist.

Buddhists   Followers of the Buddhist religion.

Capitalism   A way of running a country in which the production and distribution of goods and resources is in the hands of private businesses which aim to make profits.

Commonwealth of Independent States (CIS)   A group of eleven of the USSR's former republics which have close contacts despite being separate countries.

Communism   A way of running a country in which everything belongs to the state, and the government decides how it will be used. The wealth produced by industry and agriculture is supposed to benefit everybody in the country. The government is controlled by one political party, the Communist Party.

Coniferous forests   Forests of certain evergreen trees, such as pines, firs, cedars and redwoods, known as conifers.

Constitution   The laws about how a country is governed.

Dachas   The Russian name for weekend cottages in the country.

Democracy   A country with many political parties from which people can choose the government and Parliament in elections. People have more freedom in a democracy than under communism.

Eastern Bloc   The former communist countries of eastern Europe: Poland, Hungary, Bulgaria, Romania and the old East Germany, Czechoslovakia and Yugoslavia.

Endangered species   A particular type of animal that is in danger of dying out.

Extinction   The state of being extinct: when a type of animal has died out completely.

Five-Year Plans   Plans for the development of the economy of the USSR, each of which would take five years to complete.

Glasnost   The Russian word for being more open and truthful.

Government   The group of people elected to run a country.

Grammar   The correct use of words in speaking or writing.

Kindergarten   A school for very young children.

Latin   The language of the ancient Roman Empire.

Market economy   Businesses making what people want, rather than the government deciding what should be available in shops, as happens under communism with a command economy.

Muslims   Followers of the religion Islam and the teaching of the Prophet Muhammad.

Nomadic   Describing peoples who move from place to place to find grazing for their animals.

Perestroika   A Russian word which means 'doing things in a different way'. It is used to describe the plan to reform the economic and political structure of Russia.

Permafrost   Ground where the lower layers of soil remain frozen all year. Only the top layers of soil thaw during the summer.

Pickle   To store vegetables in vinegar to prevent them going bad.

Refugees   People who have fled from some problem or danger, such as a war.

Republic   A country, or a region within a country, with a president and government and no king or queen.

Revolution   A rising of a people against those in power.

Rodents   Small mammals that have long front teeth for gnawing (e.g. rats, mice, squirrels).

Samovar A metal urn with a tube down the centre containing burning wood. It is used to heat water for tea.

Sauna A steam bath in which you sweat yourself clean.

Slav A member of a group of peoples who originally lived in central and eastern Europe in the first century. Most of the people living in Russia today are descendants of Slavs.

Socialist Realism The official art of the Communist Party, celebrating communism and ordinary people.

Steppe Grassy, unforested plains, especially in south-east Europe and Siberia.

Taiga A region of forests. Most of the trees are coniferous.

Time zones The world is divided into 24 regions or time zones, each with a different time of day. This makes sure that everywhere in the world has noon when the sun is at its highest over each region.

Tsar The Russian word for emperor. An empress is a tsarina.

Tundra A flat, treeless region, mostly within the Arctic Circle, which is frozen for most of the year.

Vocabulary The words of a language.

Books to read

Children of the World: USSR by Julie and Robert Brown, Susan Taylor-Boyd and Susan Reitci (editors) (Gareth Stevens Children's Books, 1990)
Focus on Russia and the Republics by Elizabeth Roberts (Evans Brothers, 1992)
People and Places: USSR by Ludmilla Lewis and Marilyn Tolhurst (Macmillan, 1988)

The Russian Revolution by David Flint (Aladdin, 1993)
World in View: Soviet Union by Deborah Tyler (Heinemann, 1991)
The Volga by David Cumming (Wayland, 1994)

Picture acknowledgements

All the photographs in this book were taken by David Cumming with the exception of the following: Bruce Coleman 9 (top/Rod Williams), 9 (bottom/Dr Eckart Pott); Impact Photos 18 (bottom/Youri Lunkov), 21 (top/John Denham), 22 (bottom/B Babanov), 25 (top/Peter Arkell), 26 (top/Peter Arkell), 33 (top/Victoria Ivleva); John Massey Stewart 7, 23, 32, 41 (bottom); Peter Newark's Historical Pictures 10, 11 (both); Rex Features 13 (Roman Poderni White), 43 (left/Kevin C Frayer); Wayland Picture Library 8 (both/Anthony Lambert).

Index